Frederick Douglass

Leader of the Abolitionist Movement

Melissa Carosella

Consultant
Marcus McArthur, Ph.D.
Department of History
Saint Louis University

Publishing Credits
Dona Herweck Rice, *Editor-in-Chief*
Lee Aucoin, *Creative Director*
Chris McIntyre, M.A.Ed., *Editorial Director*
Torrey Maloof, *Associate Editor*
Neri Garcia, *Senior Designer*
Stephanie Reid, *Photo Researcher*
Rachelle Cracchiolo, M.S.Ed., *Publisher*

Image Credits
cover Alamy; p.1 Alamy; p.4 The Library of Congress; p.5 (top) The Library of Congress; p.5 (bottom) The Library of Congress; p.6 Harriet Beecher Stowe, George Cruikshank/J. Cassell, 1852/Google Books; p.7 Northwind Picture Archives; p.8 The Granger Collection, New York; p.9 (top) The Granger Collection, New York; p.9 (bottom) The Library of Congress; p.10 (left) The Library of Congress; p.10 (right) The Library of Congress; p. 11 The Library of Congress; p.12 The Granger Collection, New York; p.13 (top) The Granger Collection, New York; p.13 (bottom) The Library of Congress; p.14 (left) The Library of Congress; p.14 (right) *Life and Times of Frederick Douglass* by Frederick Douglass, Park Publishing, 1882/archive.org; p.15 (left) The Library of Congress; p.15 (right) The Library of Congress; p.16 Newscom; p.17 (top) Northwind Picture Archives; p.17 (bottom) Newscom; p.18 The Library of Congress; p.19 *Narrative of the Life of Frederick Douglass: an American Slave*, Frederick Douglass 1846/archive.org; pp.20–21 The Granger Collection, New York; p.21 The Library of Congress; p.22 The Library of Congress; p.23 The Library of Congress; p.24 The Library of Congress; p.25 The Granger Collection, New York; p.26 (left) The Library of Congress; p.26 (right) The Library of Congress; p.27 The Library of Congress; p.28 The Library of Congress; p.29 (top) National Park Service; p.29 (bottom) Getty Images; p.32 (left) The Library of Congress; p.32 (right) The Granger Collection, New York

---

Teacher Created Materials
5301 Oceanus Drive
Huntington Beach, CA 92649-1030
http://www.tcmpub.com

ISBN 978-1-4333-1518-3

Printed by: 590835
Printed in: China

Table of Contents

A Lifetime of Work

The people stood up and clapped. They were so **impressed** by what they had heard! It was 1841, and a young man named Frederick Douglass had just told 500 people about his life as a slave.

When he was a child, his family was torn apart by slavery. Slave owners hurt him. He saw how awful slavery was. He worked hard to end slavery. He wanted all slaves to be free, including himself.

Douglass began giving speeches that told people what slavery was like. He was living proof that slaves were people and not **property**. He **published** his own newspaper. He wrote books about his life. Douglass even became friends with President Lincoln!

Douglass meeting with President Lincoln

Illustration showing a slave in chains

A New Name

He was born Frederick Augustus Washington Bailey. But, after he escaped to New York in 1838, Douglass changed his name. He did not want his master to find him. From that day on, he was known as Frederick Douglass.

Speak Up!

Some slave owners lied and said that slavery was not as bad as people thought. They said that they took good care of their slaves and treated them well. But slaves who ran away told different stories. They hoped their true stories would help teach people about the evils of slavery.

Throughout his life, Douglass fought against slavery. He wanted to help all African Americans. He thought African Americans deserved equal treatment. He did everything he could to help them reach **equality**.

Frederick Douglass was born a slave, but he died a free man. He helped stop slavery and gave African Americans a chance at a better life.

Frederick Douglass

A son is taken from his mother and sold.

Growing Up a Slave

Born into Tragedy

Frederick Douglass was born in a slave cabin in Maryland. He was most likely born in 1818, but the exact year of his birth is not known. Douglass's mother was a slave named Harriet. It is not known who his father was. Some people believe Douglass's father was a white man and maybe even his owner.

Before Douglass turned a year old, his mother was sent to work on another farm miles away. She was not allowed to visit him. It was against the rules. Douglass only saw his mother a few times after she was sent away. He did not remember much about his mother. She died when Douglass was only seven years old.

How Old Am I?

When slaves were born, their owners did not record their births. No official records were kept. Because of this, many slaves did not know the year they were born or how old they were.

Left Alone

One of the worst things about slavery was that families could not always stay together. Slave owners could sell their slaves whenever they wanted. Many masters did not worry about their slaves' feelings. They only cared about making money.

Douglass was taken care of by his grandparents when he was young. Their names were Isaac and Betsey Bailey. Douglass loved his grandmother dearly.

When Douglass was about eight years old, his grandmother was ordered to take him to another farm on the **plantation**. Douglass was now old enough to start working. It was a long walk to the farm. When they got there, Douglass could not believe all the activity. Everyone was busy, and it was very loud. He wanted to go back with his grandmother. But when he went to find her, she was gone. Douglass was left all alone. Douglass's grandmother did not want to leave him, but she had to do what her master told her to do.

Slaves hard at work on a plantation

A New Outlook on Life

In 1825, Douglass was given to a new master. He was forced to leave the plantation and move to the city of Baltimore. He lived there with his old master's relatives, Hugh and Sophia Auld. Douglass liked living in the city. It was during this time that he learned to read. He also met **abolitionists** (ab-uh-LISH-uh-nists). These were people who thought slavery was wrong and worked to end it.

When Douglass first arrived, Sophia was nice and caring toward him. He had never been treated that way by a white person. She started teaching Douglass the alphabet. When she saw what a quick learner he was, she started to teach him how to read. But then things began to change for Douglass.

Mrs. Auld teaches a young Douglass the alphabet.

Douglass enjoyed spending time at Baltimore's wharf.

Hugh told his wife to stop teaching Douglass. He did not think slaves should know how to read. He believed this would make them long for freedom and be unruly, or hard to control. Sophia stopped. She also began treating Douglass like a slave. She was not as kind to him as she had once been.

Even though the Aulds began to treat him differently, Douglass still liked living in Baltimore. He secretly read books about **emancipation** and met with abolitionists. He was now more determined than ever to be free!

Against the Law!

It was against the law in slave states to teach slaves to read. People worried that if slaves learned to read they would be harder to control. They might find out other people were against slavery.

Women Abolitionists

There were many women who thought slavery was wrong. Sarah and Angelina Grimké (GRIM-key) did not like the idea of people owning other people. They wrote many letters about the evils of slavery. Lucretia (loo-KREE-shuh) Mott was a famous abolitionist, too. She gave many speeches against slavery.

Lucretia Mott

The Teacher

Douglass was once rented to a man named William Freeland. During his time with Freeland, Douglass taught other slaves in the area how to read. This was very dangerous, but Douglass knew how important it was for slaves to learn to read.

A Failed Plan

In 1835, Douglass decided to run away. He and other slaves made a plan to escape in a canoe on Chesapeake (CHES-uh-peek) Bay. But one of the slaves betrayed Douglass. Their plan was found out, and the slaves were caught and put in a slave jail.

Slave jail

A master whips his slave.

Back to the Plantation

When Douglass was 15 years old, Sophia died. Douglass was then given to Thomas Auld and had to go back to the plantation. Douglas did not want to return to plantation life, but he had no choice.

While Douglass was in Baltimore, he was allowed to go places by himself. His new master did not like Douglass's newfound spirit. He thought Douglass was spoiled and needed to be reminded that he was a slave.

Thomas hired Edward Covey. Covey was a **slave breaker**. A slave breaker was someone who was hired to beat, starve, and work slaves until they gave up all hope of a better life.

For almost a year, Douglass suffered greatly. He was given very little food. He was worked too much. He was beaten severely. Douglass began to give up hope.

Then one day, Douglass found the courage to fight back. He hit Covey. This was very dangerous. Slaves were never allowed to hit white people. But Covey could not tell anyone about the fight because then people would know he could not control his slaves. Covey never hit Douglass again.

A slave fights back.

Back to Baltimore

In 1836, Douglass was sent back to Baltimore to live with Hugh Auld again. At first, Douglass was lent out to an owner of a shipyard. He became an assistant to all the shipbuilders.

Life was better than it had been on the plantation, but it still was not easy. One day Douglass was beaten by white men who were **racists** (RAY-sists). They were angry they had to work with a slave. Douglass almost lost an eye in the fight.

After the beating, Douglass went to work in Hugh's shipyard. It was here that Douglass learned a **skilled trade**. He **caulked** ships. This means he filled the cracks and seams of the ship so that water would not leak in.

Douglass worked in a shipyard like this one.

Slaves escaped to freedom using the Underground Railroad.

While in Baltimore, Douglass began to meet free African American men who earned their own livings. These men **inspired** Douglass. He wanted a life of freedom, too. Douglass also met Anna Murray at this time. Her parents had been slaves, but she was free. The two fell in love.

Douglass's master started to grow **suspicious** (suh-SPISH-uhs) that Douglass was learning about freedom. One night, the two men had an argument. Douglass knew he had to escape soon if he was ever going to be free.

Train to Freedom

Many slaves ran away in the hope of finding freedom. One way slaves escaped was by using the **Underground Railroad**. The Underground Railroad was a big secret. People helped slaves escape to the North along special routes. People called **conductors** (kuhn-DUKH-torz) guided the slaves. One of the most famous conductors was a woman named Harriet Tubman. She led nearly 300 slaves to freedom.

Harriet Tubman

Helping Others

The Douglasses helped other slaves whenever they could. Their house was even a stop on the Underground Railroad. Anna was known to get up in the middle of the night to fix food for slaves who were escaping to Canada.

Why Douglass?

When the Douglasses arrived in New Bedford, the Johnson family helped them get settled. It was Mr. Johnson who gave Douglass his new name. Douglass needed a new name so that his master would not find him. Mr. Johnson was reading *Lady of the Lake* by Sir Walter Scott. He named Douglass after a knight in the book.

Douglass and his wife Anna shortly after their marriage

Sir Walter Scott

A New Beginning

Douglass Escapes to Freedom

In 1838, Douglass secretly boarded a train headed for New York. When he arrived in the city, he could not believe he was free.

Douglass was excited and scared. He was excited to be free but he also felt nervous. He had never been to New York City. He had no place to live and no food to eat. He did not know anyone. He was scared to talk to people. What if he got caught and was sent back to his master? But then Douglass met someone who offered to help him.

Douglass met David Ruggles (RUHG-uhlz). He was a free African American. He gave Douglass a safe place to stay. While staying with Ruggles, Douglass wrote to Murray and asked her to join him in New York. She did, and the two got married.

The Douglasses then moved to New Bedford, Massachusetts. In New Bedford, Douglass performed various jobs at the docks and was paid for his work. Douglass was finally making money. Anna was, too. She did laundry for other people. She also worked in a shoe factory. Frederick and Anna were happy. They were married for 44 years and had five children together.

Frederick and Anna Douglass

Time To Speak Out

The Douglass household did not have much money. Both Frederick and Anna worked hard and saved as much as they could. But there was one thing that Douglass did buy every week that changed his life. It was called *The Liberator*.

The Liberator was an abolitionist newspaper published by William Lloyd Garrison. Garrison was a famous abolitionist. He had been trying to end slavery for years. Garrison started his newspaper in 1831, seven years before Douglass escaped slavery.

Douglass and Garrison met at an antislavery meeting in 1841. Garrison was impressed with Douglass's story. He asked Douglass to join him at another meeting in Nantucket, New York.

William Lloyd Garrison's famous abolitionist newspaper

HORSE MARKET

SLAVES HORSES & OTHER CATTLE TO BE SOLD AT 12 OC.

LIBERTY

THE LIBERATOR

WILLIAM LLOYD GARRISON AND ISAAC KNAPP, PUBLISHERS. [NO

VOL. I.] [SATURDAY, AUGUST 13,

BOSTON, MASSACHUSETTS.] OUR COUNTRY IS THE WORLD—OUR COUNTRYMEN ARE MANKIND.

Douglass speaking in England about his experiences as a slave

When Douglass arrived at the meeting in New York, Garrison asked him to speak to the crowd. Douglass was nervous. There were 500 people at the meeting! He had never spoken to a crowd that big before. But Douglass was able to find the courage to tell his life story.

Douglass's speech was so great that it led to a job. The Massachusetts Anti-Slavery Society paid him to travel and give speeches against slavery.

Powerful Speeches

Some **ignorant** (IG-ner-uhnt) people thought slaves did not have feelings. They viewed slaves as animals who could not learn things like reading and writing. Douglass's speeches proved them wrong. He showed that African Americans had real emotions and were capable of learning.

One Hundred!

In 1843, the New England Anti-Slavery Society had a big idea. It wanted to hold 100 conventions to help stop slavery. The society asked Douglass to be one of the speakers at the 100 conventions. Douglass took the job.

William Lloyd Garrison

Slavery in England

In 1833, England had begun to end slavery. Many people from England supported American abolitionists. When Douglass spoke in England, the people were amazed by his story.

Frederick's Favorites

Douglass enjoyed reading his whole life. He read whenever he could. A reporter once asked Douglass to list his favorite authors. Douglass's list was long. It included such writers as William Shakespeare and Charlotte Brontë.

Extra! Extra!

Douglass not only read books and wrote one himself, he also started newspapers. One was called *The North Star.* This was because runaway slaves would use the North Star in the sky to guide them to freedom.

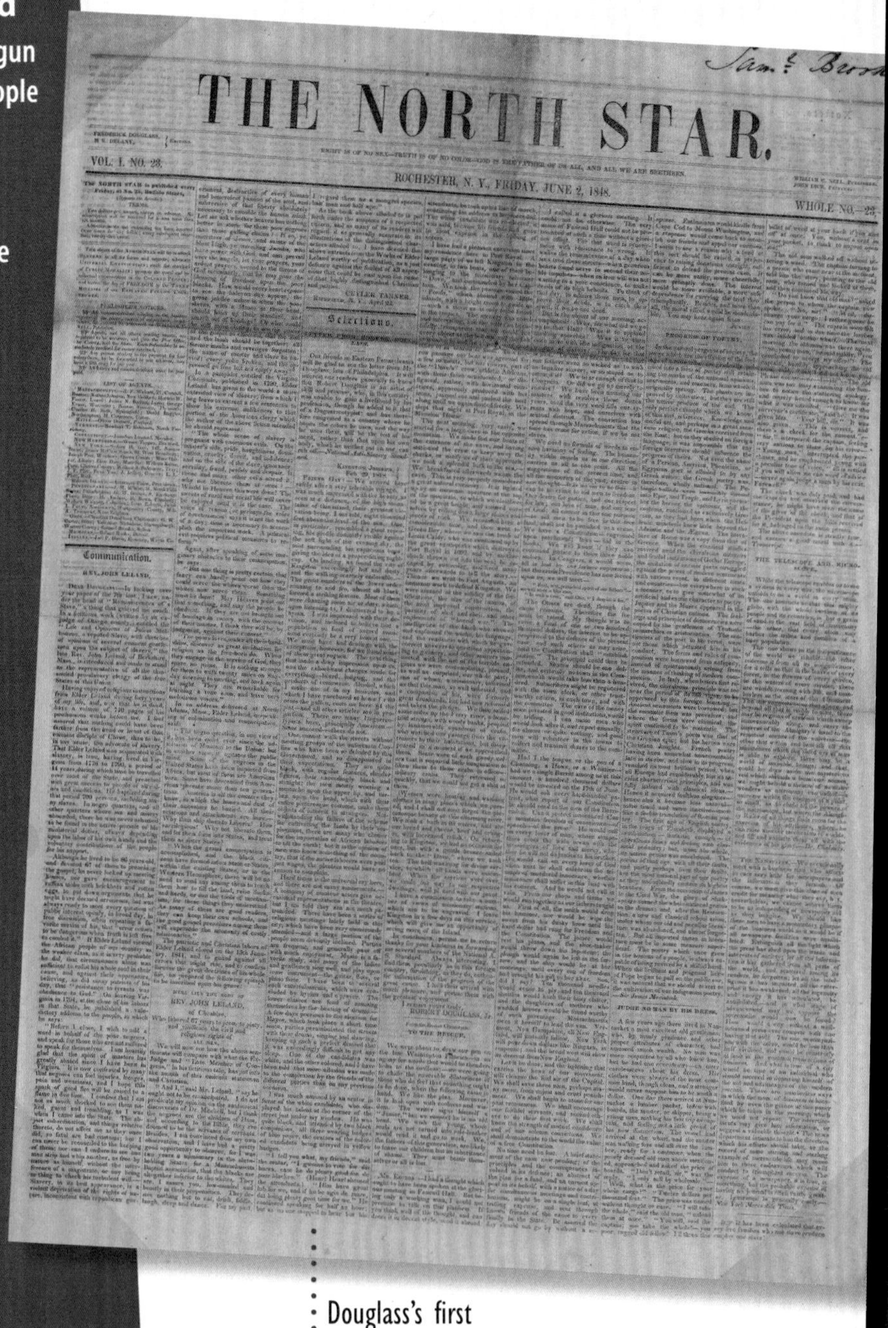

THE NORTH STAR.

VOL. I. NO. 23.

ROCHESTER, N. Y., FRIDAY, JUNE 2, 1848.

WHOLE NO.—23.

Communication.

Selections.

Douglass's first newspaper

Spreading His Ideas

Douglass believed that if people knew how horrible slavery was, they would fight to end it. In 1845, Douglass decided to write an **autobiography**. It was called *Narrative of the Life of Frederick Douglass, An American Slave.*

Douglass's friend Mr. Garrison wrote the introduction for the book. Garrison told readers that Douglass's story was true and that Douglass wrote the book himself. Many white people found it hard to believe that an African American could write so well.

When Douglass's book came out, it was a big success. It sold over 30,000 copies. Douglass was worried his old master would find him because the book was so popular. Douglass's friends told him that he should go visit Ireland and England. This way, he would be safe.

While in England, a great thing happened. English abolitionists purchased Douglass's freedom from his old master. Douglass was now legally free!

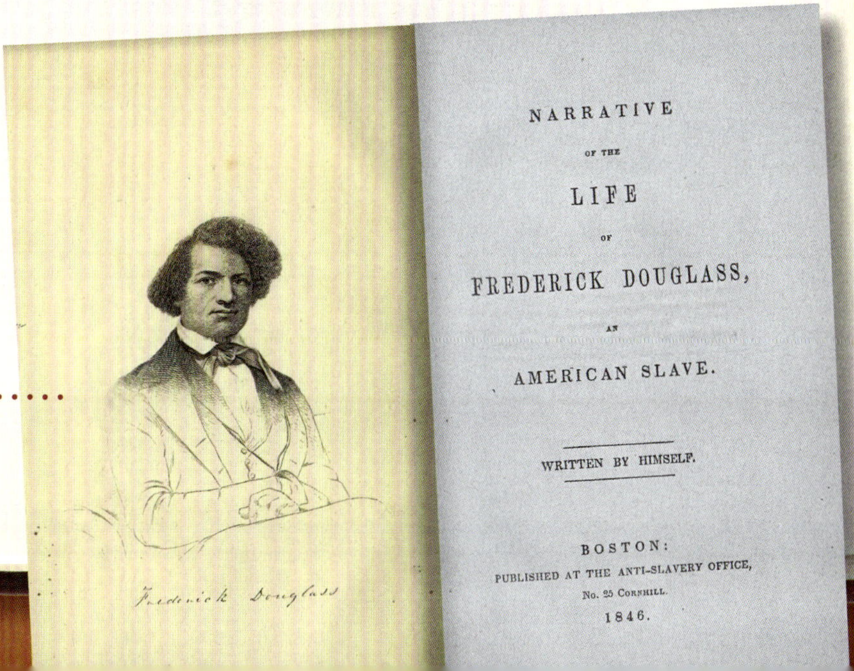

The title page of Douglass's book

A Friend in Trouble

In 1847, Douglass became friends with abolitionist John Brown. He helped Brown raise money to stop slavery. Brown hated slavery. He thought it was a sin. He would do whatever it took to end slavery. Brown thought violence was needed. But Douglass thought **politics**, not violence, could stop slavery.

In 1859, Brown started planning a slave **revolt**. He was hoping this one revolt would lead to a number of revolts throughout the South. Douglass asked Brown not to go through with this plan. Douglass was afraid the plan would not work and would anger the government.

Brown did not listen to Douglass. In October of 1859, Brown broke into an **armory** (AR-muh-ree) full of guns in Harpers Ferry, Virginia. He wanted to steal the guns and give them to slaves.

Douglass gives a speech at an antislavery meeting honoring Brown's death. Police and an angry mob try to break up the meeting.

John Brown

When the townspeople saw what Brown was doing, shots were fired. More than 17 men were killed. Brown was arrested and taken to prison.

Douglass was giving a speech when he found out Brown's plan had failed. He knew that he was in danger of being punished, too. People would think that Douglass helped Brown plan the attack because they were friends. Douglass quickly left for Canada so he would not be arrested.

Why Did They Think Douglass Was Involved?

John Brown had been planning the raid on Harpers Ferry for months. He wrote about the plans in letters to Douglass. Some of the letters were found. The letters were written proof that Douglass knew about the plan.

The Trial

Brown was put on trial for his raid on Harpers Ferry. Some people thought he had gone crazy. Others thought what he did was brave. The court found Brown guilty of **treason**, **conspiracy**, and murder. He was hanged on December 2, 1859.

Helping with the War

Douglass Finds Soldiers

In 1860, Abraham Lincoln was elected the 16th president of the United States. But the states would not stay united for long. The South did not like Lincoln. Southerners thought he wanted to end slavery. So they decided to make their own country. Lincoln did not want this. He thought the country should remain united as one. This is how the Civil War began.

The Civil War started in 1861. The North was called the Union. The South was called the Confederacy. The North fought to save the Union and to keep the country together. The South fought for the right to break apart from the union and keep their slaves.

There were many bloody battles during the war, and many soldiers died. Douglass knew the Union needed more soldiers. He thought African Americans should be able to join the army and help.

Battle at Fort Wagner

African American Civil War soldiers

One day, the governor of Massachusetts was given permission to organize a military unit consisting of African Americans. Douglass offered to help. He **recruited** African American soldiers. Douglass even recruited his own sons, Lewis and Charles. In no time, the 54th Massachusetts Infantry **Regiment** was formed. The regiment won its first battle on July 18th, 1863, at Fort Wagner. This battle showed white Union soldiers that they needed African American soldiers to help them win the war.

Only Seven Dollars!

African American soldiers were paid only $7 a month to fight for the Union. White Union soldiers made almost twice that amount. The 54th Massachusetts Infantry Regiment served for a year without pay. They wanted to make a statement that unequal pay for white and African American soldiers was unfair.

Harriet Helps, Too

Harriet Tubman is famous for her hard work on the Underground Railroad. But she also helped during the Civil War. She recruited African American soldiers to fight in the war. She also served as a nurse and helped wounded soldiers.

Meeting the President

Douglass wanted slavery stopped. He wanted all slaves to be free. But President Lincoln only wanted to stop slavery from spreading to new states.

Douglass and Lincoln also disagreed about the purpose of the Civil War. Lincoln saw the war as a way to save the country from breaking apart. Douglass saw the war as a way to end slavery. But, Douglass still had hope that Lincoln would end slavery. Then, on January 1, 1863, Lincoln issued the Emancipation Proclamation. It was the first step toward freeing slaves in America.

Abraham Lincoln

iberia

ome people thought the olution to slavery was o move to Africa. In the arly 1820s, the American olonization Society started ending free African Americans o the western coast of Africa. ventually, the country of iberia was formed.

ust in Case

n 1864, the Civil War was not oing well for the North. Lincoln vas afraid the North would lose he war. He asked Douglass o make a plan to help slaves scape if the North lost the war. ouglass wrote about his plan in letter to Lincoln. The plan was ever needed.

Freed slaves crossing into Union territory following the Emancipation Proclamation

The Emancipation Proclamation said that any person held as a slave in any of the Southern states was now free. But the slaves in the border states were not freed. Border states were the slave states that bordered the free states. Even though Lincoln had not freed all the slaves, Douglass was still hopeful that everyone would soon be free.

In 1863, Douglass got to meet with Lincoln at the White House. Douglass was impressed with the president. He found him to be an honest and trustworthy man. Lincoln and Douglass worked together during the Civil War. Douglass offered the president advice.

Hate Groups

Not all people were happy about African Americans being free. Some people started hate groups. The Ku Klux Klan (KKK) is one of those groups. The groups wanted to scare African Americans away from voting and using their new rights.

Women's Suffrage

The fight to change the law to allow women to vote was called the Suffrage Movement. Douglass was a big supporter of this movement. He believed women should have the same political rights as men. He gave many speeches on this topic and worked with the famous **suffragists** Elizabeth Cady Stanton and Susan B. Anthony.

Elizabeth Cady Stanton

A former slave celebrates his freedom.

Moving Past Slavery

Fighting for Equal Rights

The Civil War ended in April 1865. The Union had won. Then in December, the Thirteenth **Amendment** to the United States Constitution made slavery **illegal**. All slaves were now free! But Douglass wanted more. He believed that freedom meant equal rights for African Americans, not just the end of slavery.

Douglass felt that the best way to protect newly freed slaves was to pass laws giving them power. This happened in July 1868 with the Fourteenth Amendment to the U.S. Constitution. It said that slaves were citizens of the United States. Two years later, the Fifteenth Amendment gave African American men the right to vote. These amendments meant African Americans were moving closer to equal rights, as Douglass had hoped. But he knew there was still a long way to go.

Douglass wanted equal rights for everyone. He wanted African Americans to have the same rights as white men. Douglass also believed women should have these rights. Later in his life, he strove to get equal rights for **immigrants**, too. Douglass believed that everyone should be treated equally regardless of their race, gender, or nationality.

Freedmen, or former slaves, voting in the South in 1867

From Slave to Legend

Douglass worked hard his whole life. In 1881, Douglass took a job working for the government. He was the recorder of deeds in Washington, DC. He kept track of important papers for the government.

A few years later, Douglass was **appointed** consul general to Haiti (HEY-tee). This meant that he represented the United States government in Haiti. Haiti used to be a slave country. But the slaves fought their masters. They won control of the country. Douglass lived in Haiti until 1891.

When Douglass returned to the United States, he continued to fight for equality for all. On February 20, 1895, Douglass spoke at a meeting supporting equal rights for women. After that meeting, he became sick. Douglass died later that day at the age of 77.

Frederick Douglass was born a slave. The law did not consider him a person. It said he was someone's property. Douglass risked his life many times to change that law. His hard work and brave spirit helped set the United States on a path toward equality for all its citizens.

African Americans pay their respects to Douglass in 1877.

Helen Pitts

A Second Wife

Anna Douglass died in 1882, and Douglass was very lonely. In 1884, he married Helen Pitts. She was about 20 years younger than Douglass. She was also white. Many people disapproved of the marriage, but it did not matter. Frederick and Helen Douglass were happy.

Home Sweet Home

In 1878, Douglass moved to a house in Cedar Hill, Anacostia, in Washington, DC. This is where he lived with his family until his death in 1895. Today, the very house Douglass lived in is a museum. It is run by the National Park Service. The home even has some of Douglass's personal belongings. The home is open to the public. This means you can tour Douglass's home!

Douglass appeared on the cover of *LIFE* magazine in 1968, more than 70 years after he died.

Glossary

abolitionists—people who fight to end slavery

amendment—an official change to the United States Constitution

appointed—given a job in the government

armory—a place where arms, or weapons, are kept

autobiography—a book about a person's life written by that person

caulked—filled in cracks or seams in ships so that water cannot leak in

conductors—people who led slaves to freedom using the Underground Railroad

conspiracy—a secret, unlawful act

emancipation—freedom from slavery

equality—when everyone gets the same treatment; when people are equal

ignorant—not knowing much about something; refusing to learn

illegal—against the law

immigrants—people who come to a country to live there

impressed—to have done a good job; to have made people notice your work

inspired—made someone else want to be like you

plantation—a large house on a huge piece of land, usually located in the South

politics—guiding or influencing government policies

property—something that is owned like land, goods, or money

published—to have printed a book or newspaper

racists—people who judge other people by the color of their skin

recruited—got people to join

regiment—a military unit

revolt—a fight for freedom, often violent

skilled trade—a job that needs special skills

slave breaker—a person who abused slaves to make them give up hope of a better life

suffragists—people who thought women should be allowed to vote

suspicious—less trustful; feeling that something strange is going on

treason—the crime of fighting against your country's government

Underground Railroad—a secret system that helped slaves escape to freedom in the North or Canada

Index

Your Turn!

Frederick Douglass showed the world that slaves had feelings and dreams, just like everyone else. He bravely told his story and helped end slavery in America.

Poetic Persona

Use what you know about Frederick Douglass to write an "I am" poem. On a separate sheet of paper, fill in the blanks to tell his story in poem form.

I am ______________________________

I see ______________________________

I feel ______________________________

I say ______________________________

I believe ____________________________

I am ______________________________